21 Prayers
for Teen Girls!

Shelley Hitz and Heather Hart

21 Prayers for Teen Girls!

Shelley Hitz and Heather Hart

© 2013 Body and Soul Publishing
Printed In the United States of America

ISBN-13: 978-0615918280
ISBN-10: 061591828X

Scripture quotations marked NIV are taken from the Holy Bible, New International Version® 1973, 1978, 1984 by International Bible Society. Used by permission of Zondervan Publishing House. All rights reserved.

Scripture quotations marked NKJV are taken from the Holy Bible, New King James Version®. Copyright © 1982 by Thomas Nelson, Inc. Used by permission. All rights reserved.

Scripture quotations marked NLT are taken from the Holy Bible, New Living Translation, copyright 1996, 2004. Used by permission of Tyndale House Publishers, Inc., Wheaton, Illinois 60189. All rights reserved.

Scripture quotations marked AMP are taken from the Amplified® Bible, Copyright © 1954, 1958, 1962, 1964, 1965, 1987 by The Lockman Foundation Used by permission. All rights reserved. (www.Lockman.org)

Scripture quotations marked ESV are taken from The Holy Bible, English Standard Version® (ESV®), copyright © 2001 by Crossway, a publishing ministry of Good News Publishers. Used by permission. All rights reserved.

Scripture quotations marked "KJV" are taken from the Holy Bible, King James Version, Cambridge, 1769.

Scripture quotations marked NASB are taken from the New American Standard Bible®, Copyright © 1960, 1962, 1963, 1968, 1971, 1972, 1973, 1975, 1977, 1995 by The Lockman Foundation. Used by permission. (www.Lockman.org)

Presented to:

From:

Date:

CONTENTS

INTRODUCTION

Heather Hart

You've heard that it takes 21 days to form a new habit, right?

Lots of people spend 21 days trying not to drink soda, to form a new exercise routine, or even to stop cussing.

Why not take 21 days to form a habit of praying for our true beauty? Praying to be the women that God created us to be.

In a world that idolizes outer beauty, we need to look to our Creator to find our true beauty, and there's no better way to do that than to develop a habit that will draw us closer to Christ.

This book holds 21 prayers you can pray to become more beautiful in Christ. But you need to know that these prayers weren't written just for you; first and foremost these are our prayers, to our Father. We don't just want you to look to Him for your true beauty, we look to Him ourselves.

So what do you say? Will you join us in praying for our true beauty?

~~*~*~*

"And pray in the Spirit on all occasions with all kinds of prayers and requests. With this in mind, be alert and always keep on praying for all the Lord's people."

~ Ephesians 6:18 (NIV)

"Be joyful in hope, patient in affliction, faithful in prayer."
~Romans 12:12 (NIV)

"Never stop praying."
~ 1 Thessalonians 5:17 (NLT)

"Hear my prayer, O God; listen to the words of my mouth."
~ Psalm 54:2 (NASB)

PRAYER #1:
TRUE BEAUTY

Shelley Hitz

Lord, I thank You that I am fearfully and wonderfully made. You created me and knit me together in my mother's womb. However, some days I struggle. I don't feel good enough or pretty enough and I start to believe the lies of the enemy.

Empower me through Your Holy Spirit to find my value and worth in You. Help me to replace the lies of the enemy with Your Truth that I am a new creation in Christ... the old has gone and the new has come. I praise You that my true beauty is not in my outer appearance, but is found in who I am in Christ. I love You so much. Amen.

"For You formed my inward parts; You covered me in my mother's womb. I will praise You, for I am fearfully and wonderfully made; Marvelous are Your works, And that my soul knows very well."
~ Psalm 139: 13-14 (NKJV)

"My old self has been crucified with Christ. It is no longer I who live, but Christ lives in me. So I live in this earthly body by trusting in the Son of God, who loved me and gave himself for me."
~ Galatians 2:20 (NLT)

PRAYER #2:
REFLECTION

Heather Hart

Lord God, please help me to be a living reflection of You. When others look at me, I don't want them to see who I am on the surface. I don't want to be seen as a reflection of my appearance, my grades, or even extracurricular activities that I do, Lord. I want others to see You living in me.

I want to live a life that reflects what Christ did for me on the cross on a daily basis, God. I want my life to be a witness for You – living daily to display Your grace, mercy, and all around beauty.

I also know that this isn't something that I can do on my own, Lord. I need You. I need You to live in me and through me so that I can reflect Your beauty. I need You living in my heart, not just my head, Lord. Please help me, I pray.

"As in water face reflects face, So the heart of man reflects man."
~ Proverbs 27:19 (NASB)

4

"Beloved, now we are children of God, and it has not appeared as yet what we will be. We know that when He appears, we will be like Him, because we will see Him just as He is."

~ 1 John 3:2 (NASB)

"Therefore, I urge you, brothers and sisters, in view of God's mercy, to offer your bodies as a living sacrifice, holy and pleasing to God—this is your true and proper worship. Do not conform to the pattern of this world, but be transformed by the renewing of your mind. Then you will be able to test and approve what God's will is—his good, pleasing and perfect will."

~ Romans 12:1-2 (NIV)

"I want to know Christ—yes, to know the power of his resurrection and participation in his sufferings, becoming like him in his death, and so, somehow, attaining to the resurrection from the dead."

~ Philippians 3:10-11 (NIV)

PRAYER #3:
PURITY

Shelley Hitz

Lord, I come to You today asking for You to purify me from the inside out through Your Holy Spirit. Crucify my flesh and any of my desires that are not from You. I am pressured daily by my friends and the media to conform to this world. However, I want to live for You and not for myself. I ask You to transform me through the renewing of my mind.

I acknowledge that as a follower of Christ, my body is not my own... it is a temple of the Holy Spirit. Empower me to honor You with my body in every way – by the way I dress, the way I act, the things I say, and through my actions. Purify me, Lord. I need You desperately. Amen.

"I beseech you therefore, brethren, by the mercies of God, that you present your bodies a living sacrifice, holy, acceptable to God, which is your reasonable service. And do not be conformed to this world, but be transformed by the renewing of your mind, that you may prove what is that good and acceptable and perfect will of God."

~ Romans 12:1-2 (NKJV)

"Run from sexual sin! No other sin so clearly affects the body as this one does. For sexual immorality is a sin against your own body. Don't you realize that your body is the temple of the Holy Spirit, who lives in you and was given to you by God? You do not belong to yourself, for God bought you with a high price. So you must honor God with your body."

~ I Corinthians 6:18-20 (NLT)

PRAYER #4:
DILIGENCE

Heather Hart

Father God, please help me to stay on task today. There are so many things that I want to do – and so many things I don't. Help me to do what needs to be done.

Help me to push forward in the directions that You want me to go and to work hard – bringing You glory and honor. I know that as a Christian my work ethic reflects on You whether I intend it to or not. So when I slack off, I'm not just being lazy, Lord, but a bad witness as well. I don't always think about it like that, but it's true.

Please remind me as I go about my day that I am Your representative. Give me the strength I need to work hard and point me towards the tasks that I need to be working on. Be my guide and my strength I pray. Amen.

"Therefore, my beloved brethren, be steadfast, immovable, always abounding in the work of the Lord, knowing that your toil is not in vain in the Lord."

~ 1 Corinthians 15:58 (NASB)

"All hard work brings a profit, but mere talk leads only to poverty."

~ Proverbs 14:23 (NIV)

"Never be lacking in zeal, but keep your spiritual fervor, serving the Lord."

~ Romans 12:11 (NIV)

"Sow your seed in the morning and do not be idle in the evening, for you do not know whether morning or evening sowing will succeed, or whether both of them alike will be good."

~ Ecclesiastes 11:6 (NASB)

PRAYER #5:
ACCEPTED

Shelley Hitz

Lord, I thank You that I am accepted in You. In both little and big ways I am often rejected by my friends, family or others. The only person I can depend on completely that will NEVER let me down is You. Everyone else in my life is imperfect. Therefore they will reject me or disappoint me at some point in our relationship. However, I can put my full trust in You because You never change. You are the same yesterday, today and forever.

I often need the reminder that there is no condemnation in Christ Jesus.

I am accepted in You.

When I confess my sins to You, Jesus, You forgive me completely and remember my sins no more. They are gone. Help me to walk in Your forgiveness and acceptance today. Amen.

"Blessed be the God and Father of our Lord Jesus Christ, who hath blessed us with all spiritual blessings in heavenly places in Christ: according as He hath chosen us in Him before the foundation of the world, that we should be holy and without blame before Him

in love: having predestinated us unto the adoption of children by Jesus Christ to Himself, according to the good pleasure of His will, to the praise of the glory of His grace, wherein He hath made us **accepted in the beloved.**"

~ Ephesians 1:3-6 (KJV)

"Jesus Christ is the same yesterday, today, and forever."

~ Hebrews 13:8 (NKJV)

"There is therefore now no condemnation to those who are in Christ Jesus, who do not walk according to the flesh, but according to the Spirit."

~ Romans 8:1 (NKJV)

"For I will forgive their wickedness and will remember their sins no more."

~ Hebrews 8:12 (NIV)

PRAYER #6:
HUMILITY

Heather Hart

Father God, today I pray for humility. I pray that You will help me to see that it is only through You that I can accomplish anything – and that it is only You who are worthy of praise.

Lord, help me not to exalt myself, or to look down on others. Help me to humbly serve You and love those around me.

Let me not judge or display a spirit of pride, instead, let me remember You reign on high over all, and love us all the same.

Give me a spirit of humility and love this day I pray; Amen.

"Have this attitude in yourselves which was also in Christ Jesus, who, although He existed in the form of God, did not regard equality with God a thing to be grasped, but emptied Himself, taking the form of a bond-servant, and being made in the likeness of men. Being found in appearance as a man, He humbled Himself by becoming obedient to the point of death, even death on a cross."
~ Philippians 2:5-8 (NASB)

"Indeed, there is not a righteous man on earth who continually does good and who never sins."
~ Ecclesiastes 7:20 (NASB)

"Whatever happens, conduct yourselves in a manner worthy of the gospel of Christ. Then, whether I come and see you or only hear about you in my absence, I will know that you stand firm in the one Spirit, striving together as one for the faith of the gospel"
~ Philippians 1:27 (NIV)

"This righteousness is given through faith in Jesus Christ to all who believe. There is no difference between Jew and Gentile, for all have sinned and fall short of the glory of God, and all are justified freely by His grace through the redemption that came by Christ Jesus."
~ Romans 3:22-24 (NIV)

PRAYER #7: GOSSIP

Shelley Hitz

Lord, my words often get me in trouble. It is so easy to get caught up in talking about others in a negative way that tears them down instead of building them up. Sometimes I simply need to keep quiet and not say anything at all if I can't say something good about the situation or person.

I confess my sin of gossip to You and ask You to forgive me. Empower me to change so that my words may be acceptable in Your sight. Give me strength to be different than those around me in every way, even in my conversations and the words I speak. May I be a person that encourages many through my words. Amen.

~~*~*~*

"So also the tongue is a small member, yet it boasts of great things. How great a forest is set ablaze by such a small fire! And the tongue is a fire, a world of unrighteousness. The tongue is set among our members, staining the whole body, setting on fire the entire course of life, and set on fire by hell."
~ James 3:5-6 (ESV)

"Too much talk leads to sin. Be sensible and keep your mouth shut...The words of the godly encourage many."
~ Proverbs 10:19, 21a (NKJV)

"A gossip betrays a confidence; so avoid anyone who talks too much."

~ Proverbs 20:19 (NIV)

"Let the words of my mouth and the meditation of my heart be acceptable in Your sight, O Lord, my strength and my Redeemer."

~ Psalm 19:14 (NKJV)

PRAYER #8:
LOVE

Heather Hart

Fill me with Your love, oh God. Fill me to the full so that Your love will flow out of me to those I come in contact with. Lord, I often find it hard to love others in both spirit and in truth – I judge, I hate, I covet. I'm a fallen, sinful human. Help me to love others, Lord.

Help me to love my family and peers with a love that comes from You. Help me to love them unconditionally and not be bested by my temper. Help me not to get in the way of letting Your love shine through me. The love You displayed so well when You sent Your Son, Jesus Christ, to die for me – and to die for them.

Let my actions be driven by love, not selfishness.

Let my word be encouragement and a benefit to those around me – words spoken in love, not haste.

Let my thoughts be filled with kindness, fueled by Your love overflowing in me.

Help me to love others today, Lord, I pray. Amen.

~~*~*~*

"Let all that you do be done in love."

$\sim$ 1 Corinthians 16:14 (NASB)

"Share with the Lord's people who are in need. Practice hospitality."

$\sim$ Romans 12:13 (NIV)

See Also 1 Corinthians 13

PRAYER #9:
CHERISHED

Shelley Hitz

Dear Lord, I thank You that I am loved and cherished by You. Many people do things for me to show me their love. But nothing compares to You sending Your Son to take away my sins. Thank You for showing Your *wonderful and intense love* to me in this way. It simply amazes me.

Not only do You love me with an unconditional love, but You rejoice over me with singing. Thank You, Father, for loving me in such a complete way. Sometimes I crave the love and attention that a guy can give me. But ultimately I know that I will only be satisfied in Your love. Help me to truly know and understand Your great love for me and how much You cherish me today. I love You! Amen.

"This is real love—not that we loved God, but that He loved us and sent His Son as a sacrifice to take away our sins."
~ 1 John 4:10 (NLT)

*"But God—so rich is He in His mercy! Because of and in order to satisfy the great and wonderful and **intense love** with which He loved us, even when we were dead (slain) by [our own]*

shortcomings and trespasses, He made us alive together in fellowship and in union with Christ."

~ Ephesians 2:4-5a (AMP)

"The Lord your God in your midst, the Mighty One, will save; He will rejoice over you with gladness, He will quiet you with His love, He will rejoice over you with singing."

~Zephaniah 3:17 (NKJV)

PRAYER #10:
PEER PRESSURE

Heather Hart

Father God, I desire to dedicate my life to You. I want You to be my focus – my everything. I'm really excited about some of the things going on in my life - my friends, some of the projects I'm working on, etc. - but at the same time, I don't want them to distract me from You.

James 1:27 says *"...to keep oneself from being polluted by the world."* But Lord, that's hard. We live in a world full of pollution. Physically people throw trash out of car windows, cars leak oil, and then there is cigarette smoke. It all works together with hundreds of other things to pollute Your world.

...but the worst pollution of all is the emotional and spiritual pollution. We're surrounded at school and work by filthy language. We're invited to go places we know we shouldn't be. We're enticed to watch shows on T.V. that not only don't honor You, but pollute our minds against You without us even realizing it. It's often referred to as peer pressure, but it goes so much deeper than that. There's the pressure from our friends to do what's fun, pressure from the media to look good, and then the pressure that we put on ourselves to have fun and be somebody.

I'm guilty of giving into that pressure, Lord. I'm guilty of being polluted by the world. I find it easier to give in than to stand strong for You. But today You reminded me of what we're taught at school about pollution – we can either be part of the problem, or we can work against it. We might not be able to stop it all together, but we can do our best. I want to do my best for You, Lord.

I don't want to be part of the world's pollution. I don't want to bring others down spiritually or emotionally or add pollution to someone else's mind (or even my own). I want to stand up for You and my faith and work towards having a spiritually clean environment. Help me to stand strong for You, Lord, I pray. Amen.

~~*~*~*

"Am I now trying to win the approval of human beings, or of God? Or am I trying to please people? If I were still trying to please people, I would not be a servant of Christ."
~ Galatians 1:10 (NIV)

"Beloved, do not imitate what is evil, but what is good. Anyone who does what is good is from God. Anyone who does what is evil has not seen God."
~ 3 John 1:11 (NASB)

"We do not want you to become lazy, but to imitate those who through faith and patience inherit what has been promised."
~ Hebrews 6:12 (NIV)

"Pay careful attention to your own work, for then you will get the satisfaction of a job well done, and you won't need to compare yourself to anyone else. For we are each responsible for our own conduct."
~ Galatians 6:4-5 (NLT)

PRAYER #11:
DEPRESSION

Heather Hart

Lord God, You know me. You know the thoughts of my mind and the battle of my heart. You know me to the very depths of my soul. So You aren't surprised by the feelings I'm having. You're not surprised by the thoughts that pop into my mind. You know the end from the beginning – but I don't.

I'm not happy, God. I can't tell you exactly what causes this mood, I know that there are good things in my life God, but I can't get past the pain. I can't see past my failures or the things that are going wrong to trust in You. I know I should, but it's hard, God.

Help me to trust in You. Help me to look past myself, past today, to see the bigger picture that You have planned for me. Lord, I know that all things are possible for those who love You – and I do love You. Please lift my spirits and help me to soar on wings like an eagle – singing Your praises with a joyful heart.

~~*~*~*

"Yet those who wait for the Lord will gain new strength; They will mount up with wings like eagles, They will run and not get tired, They will walk and not become weary."

~ Isaiah 40:31 (NASB)

"And we know that God causes all things to work together for good to those who love God, to those who are called according to His purpose."

~ Romans 8:28 (NASB)

"Therefore we do not lose heart. Though outwardly we are wasting away, yet inwardly we are being renewed day by day. For our light and momentary troubles are achieving for us an eternal glory that far outweighs them all. So we fix our eyes not on what is seen, but on what is unseen, since what is seen is temporary, but what is unseen is eternal."

~ 2 Corinthians 4:16-18 (NIV)

PRAYER #12:
RESPECT

Shelley Hitz

Lord, thank You for the people You have placed in my life. Thank You for my friends, family, teachers, neighbors, etc. Help me to shine Christ through my life to them. One way I do this is by treating everyone with respect and honor.

However, there are certain people in my life that are difficult to love. I know that I can only love them through the empowering of Your Holy Spirit that lives within me. Help me to respond to my enemies with love instead of hate. In doing this, You will shine brightly through my life.

I need to die to my own selfishness, pride and my flesh. It is so easy to be self-centered and focus on what is best for ME. Help me to live a humble life where I consider others better than myself. I love You, Lord! Amen.

"Show respect for all men [treat them honorably]. Love the brotherhood (the Christian fraternity of which Christ is the Head). Reverence God. Honor the emperor."

~I Peter 2:17 (AMP)

"You have heard the law that says, 'Love your neighbor' and hate your enemy. But I say, love your enemies! Pray for those who persecute you! In that way, you will be acting as true children of your Father in heaven. For He gives His sunlight to both the evil and the good, and He sends rain on the just and the unjust alike. If you love only those who love you, what reward is there for that? Even corrupt tax collectors do that much. If you are kind only to your friends, how are you different from anyone else? Even pagans do that. But you are to be perfect, even as your Father in heaven is perfect."

~ Matthew 5:43-48 (NLT)

"Let nothing be done through selfish ambition or conceit, but in lowliness of mind let each esteem others better than himself."

~ Philippians 2:3 (NKJV)

PRAYER #13:
ANGER

Heather Hart

Lord, You are a holy, righteous, and yet gentle God. People sin against You every moment of everyday – myself included. Yet You are slow to anger. You are filled with mercy and grace. Help me to be more like You.

When people sin against me, or when things just don't go my way, I pray that you remind me of Your mercy – Your forgiveness. Help me to respond with that same merciful spirit and not a spirit of anger. Help me to be slow to anger and quick to love.

Help me to not respond to others in anger, but to stop and think and pray. Help me to remember Your love for me and for them – and then help my response to be fueled by that love and not my own haughty spirit.

I pray this in the name of Your Son; Amen.

"...to be sensible, pure, workers at home, kind, being subject to their own husbands, so that the word of God will not be dishonored."

~ Titus 2:5 (NASB)

"A gentle answer turns away wrath, but a harsh word stirs up anger."

~ Proverbs 15:1 (NASB)

"The Lord is gracious and merciful; Slow to anger and great in lovingkindness."

~ Psalm 145:8 (NASB)

"This you know, my beloved brethren. But everyone must be quick to hear, slow to speak and slow to anger."

~ James 1:19(NASB)

PRAYER #14: FORGIVENESS

Shelley Hitz

Dear Lord, I know that on this side of heaven I will need to come to you _continuously_ to confess my sins and ask for Your forgiveness. Just like I need to take a bath or shower on a regular basis, I also need to come to You for a spiritual cleansing on a regular basis.

I am so thankful that when I confess my sins and ask Your forgiveness, I am forgiven. You don't keep a record of my sins, but instead cast them into Your huge sea of grace where You put up a sign that says "No Fishing Allowed." :)

Today, I come to You and confess my sin of _____. I ask for You to forgive me and empower me through the Holy Spirit to truly repent from this sin. When I repent and change, people will notice. I will be different. But, I acknowledge that I can only change through Your power and Your strength. Thank You for Your amazing forgiveness and grace. I love You! Amen.

"He is faithful and just...will forgive our sins...and [continuously] cleanse us from all unrighteousness."

~ I John 1:9 (AMP)

"If You, O Lord, kept a record of sins, who could stand? But with You there is forgiveness, therefore you are feared."

~ Psalm 130:3-4 (NIV)

"I say to you that likewise there will be more joy in heaven over one sinner who repents than over ninety-nine just persons who need no repentance."

~ Luke 15:7 (NKJV)

PRAYER #15:
CONTENT

Heather Hart

Father God, life is never how I think it will be. I don't know why I haven't just accepted that yet and relinquished control to You, but I haven't. There's a scripture that says, a man can plan his own way, but You direct his steps (Proverbs 16:9). That is so true, God.

But I forget.

I forget that You are in control and I get frustrated. I get mad when things don't go my way or seem to be working against me. I get frustrated when I screw up. I need Your help.

Help me to be content in You, Lord. Help me to trust that You know what's best for my life and that You can work all things together for good (Rom. 8:28). I ask for Your peace, Lord God. And I ask in the name of Your Holy Son, Jesus Christ, my Lord and Savior. Amen.

"So do not fear, for I am with you; do not be dismayed, for I am your God. I will strengthen you and help you; I will uphold you with my righteous right hand."

~ Isaiah 41:10 (NIV)

"Make sure that your character is free from the love of money, being content with what you have; for He Himself has said, 'I will never desert you, nor will I ever forsake you,'"
~ Hebrews 13:5 (NASB)

"Not that I speak from want, for I have learned to be content in whatever circumstances I am. I know how to get along with humble means, and I also know how to live in prosperity; in any and every circumstance I have learned the secret of being filled and going hungry, both of having abundance and suffering need. I can do all things through Him who strengthens me."
~ Philippians 4:11-13 (NASB)

PRAYER #16:
FAITH

Shelley Hitz

Lord, thank You that You are not only the author of my faith but also the perfecter of my faith. I ask that You continue to perfect my faith as many times I still waver in unbelief. I confess my unbelief to You right now. As the father said to Jesus about healing his son, "I do believe; help me overcome my unbelief." I ask Your forgiveness and pray for the strength to believe in You despite my circumstances.

I also realize that without faith it is impossible to please You. Impossible. Help me to remember this when doubts slip into my mind and lies from the enemy tempt me to not believe Your promises. Strengthen me with power from Your Holy Spirit to have faith that stands the test of time.

Thank You for equipping me with the shield of faith to fight the battles that wage in my mind. With my shield of faith raised high, I can quench the fiery darts from the enemy that seek to destroy me.

And right now I affirm my faith and belief in You, Lord. I believe, I believe, I do believe! Amen.

~~*~*~*

"Let us fix our eyes on Jesus, the author and perfecter of our faith, who for the joy set before him endured the cross, scorning its shame, and sat down at the right hand of the throne of God."
~ Hebrews 12:2 (NIV)

"Immediately the boy's father exclaimed, 'I do believe; help me overcome my unbelief!'"
~ Mark 9:24 (NIV)

"But without faith it is impossible to please Him, for he who comes to God must believe that He is, and that He is a rewarder of those who diligently seek Him."
~ Hebrews 11:6 (NKJV)

"Above all, taking the shield of faith with which you will be able to quench all the fiery darts of the wicked one."
~ Ephesians 6:16 (NKJV)

Prayer #17:
Choose Wisely

Heather Hart

Abba Father, I am faced with millions of choices each day. Some are simple decisions like which pair of socks to wear or what to eat for breakfast. But others are not so easy and often have impacts I don't consider.

Help me to make the choices today that will honor You. Help me to stop and think things through – not just act on my impulses.

Lord, I know that the decisions that are best, the ones that please You and are the right path to follow, aren't always the easy ones... okay, are rarely the easy ones. Give me the strength to make those tough decisions. Help me act as Your daughter – making the choices that please You and are best for me even when they aren't easy.

"You, my brothers and sisters, were called to be free. But do not use your freedom to indulge the flesh; rather, serve one another humbly in love. For the entire law is fulfilled in keeping this one command: "Love your neighbor as yourself." If you bite and devour each other, watch out or you will be destroyed by each other."

~ Galatians 5:13-15 (NIV)

"You say, 'I am allowed to do anything'—but not everything is good for you. You say, 'I am allowed to do anything'—but not everything is beneficial."

~ 1 Corinthians 10:23 (NLT)

"Whether, then, you eat or drink or whatever you do, do all to the glory of God."

~ 1 Corinthians 10:31 (NASB)

PRAYER #18:
HONOR YOUR PARENTS

Shelley Hitz

Lord, thank You for this new day. I know that each day is a gift from You. I also thank You for the parents You have given me. They are not perfect and make mistakes, but I know that no one is perfect except for You, Jesus. Help me to honor and obey my parents, even when it is difficult and I don't agree with them. I know that You have promised me long life when I obey and honor my parents.

I pray that You would lead and guide my parents. Help them to make wise decisions so that they can give me the guidance and direction I need. May they listen to You and put You first in their lives.

Thank You for being my heavenly Father. Even when my earthly parents fall short, I know that I can fully depend on You to "father" me. Help me to be a godly example to my parents as You empower me to obey and honor them. Amen.

"Children, obey your parents in the Lord, for this is right. 'Honor your father and mother,' which is the first commandment with promise: 'that it may be well with you and you may live long on the earth.'"

~ Ephesians 6:1-3 (NKJV)

"A wise child accepts a parent's discipline; a mocker refuses to listen to correction."

~ Proverbs 13:1 (NLT)

PRAYER #19:
GOD'S WORD

Heather Hart

Father God, sometimes the Bible just doesn't seem relevant to me. I pick it up and read, but it just doesn't click. I know You long for me to read Your Word. I know it's how I ultimately deepen my relationship with You, but it is hard sometimes, Lord.

Some days it comes easily. I read one verse and You just speak to me through it – but other days there's nothing. So I ask You today, please help me to read and understand Your Word. Help me not to push aside my Bible for the newest book I've downloaded. Help me to remember how important it is in my spiritual growth. Help me to remember that it's Your love letter – to me.

I know that the Bible is true. I know that it applies to my life today – help me to understand it and to apply it to my life, Lord. Ultimately I ask that the time I spend in Your Word, would deepen my relationship with You and my true beauty in Christ.

I want to learn more about how to please You and live the life You want me to live. But I need Your help. You said that the Holy Spirit would guide me and teach me (John 14:26) – so let it be.

In the name of Your Son, Jesus Christ, I pray – Amen.

~~*~*~*

"All Scripture is inspired by God and profitable for teaching, for reproof, for correction, for training in righteousness; so that the man of God may be adequate, equipped for every good work."
~ 2 Timothy 3:16-17 (NASB)

"For you have been born again, not of perishable seed, but of imperishable, through the living and enduring word of God."
~ 1 Peter 1:23 (NIV)

"For the word of God is living and active and sharper than any two-edged sword, and piercing as far as the division of soul and spirit, of both joints and marrow, and able to judge the thoughts and intentions of the heart."
~ Hebrews 4:12 (NASB)

"And take the helmet of salvation, and the sword of the Spirit, which is the word of God."
~ Ephesians 6:17 (NASB)

"For this reason we also constantly thank God that when you received the word of God which you heard from us, you accepted it not as the word of men, but for what it really is, the word of God, which also performs its work in you who believe."
~ 1 Thessalonians 2:13 (NASB)

PRAYER #20:
PATIENCE

Shelley Hitz

Lord, thank You for Your Holy Spirit that fills me with patience. I admit that sometimes I lose my patience with the people in my life and ask for Your forgiveness.

Thank You for the opportunities You place in my life to teach me patience. Although it is difficult to walk through these circumstances at the time, I know that it builds patience and endurance within me. This helps me to grow into a mature Christian and to be complete, lacking nothing.

I can do nothing apart from You, Lord. I realize that on my own, I will never be patient. I need You to change me and empower me to be patient with the people and circumstances in my life. Amen.

"But the fruit of the Spirit is love, joy, peace, patience, kindness, goodness, faithfulness, gentleness, self-control; against such things there is no law."
~ Galatians 5:22-23 (ESV)

"We also pray that you will be strengthened with all His glorious power so you will have all the endurance and patience you need.

May you be filled with joy, always thanking the Father. He has enabled you to share in the inheritance that belongs to His people, who live in the light."

~ Colossians 1:11-12 (NLT)

"My brethren, count it all joy when you fall into various trials, knowing that the testing of your faith produces patience. But let patience have its perfect work, that you may be perfect and complete, lacking nothing."

~ James 1:2-4 (NKJV)

"I am the vine, you are the branches. He who abides in Me, and I in him, bears much fruit; for without Me you can do nothing."

~ John 15:5 (NKJV)

PRAYER #21:
DRAWING CLOSE

Heather Hart

Lord, draw me close to You, I pray. I want You to reign in my life and in my heart. I want to be more like You. I want to be a reflection of You – letting the beauty of Your love shine through me.

Draw me near to You, so I can honestly say with Paul, "*I have been crucified with Christ; and it is no longer I who live, but Christ lives in me; and the life which I now live in the flesh I live by faith in the Son of God, who loved me and gave Himself up for me.*" (Gal 2:20 NASB)

Keep me within Your grasp – hold me close to You, Lord. Change my heart and renew my spirit. Not just today, Lord, but every day.

Cover me with Your grace, and help my desire to be for You alone. Surround me with Your love and reign over my heart today and always.

In the name of Your Holy and Righteous Son – my Savior – I pray; Amen.

~~*~*~*

"Therefore let us draw near with confidence to the throne of grace, so that we may receive mercy and find grace to help in time of need."
~ Hebrews 4:16 (NASB)

"Let us draw near with a true heart in full assurance of faith, with our hearts sprinkled clean from an evil conscience and our bodies washed with pure water."
~ Hebrews 10:22 (ESV)

"Draw near to God and He will draw near to you. Cleanse your hands, you sinners; and purify your hearts, you double-minded."
~ James 4:8 (NASB)

"But he who is joined to the Lord becomes one spirit with him."
~ 1 Corinthians 6:17 (ESV)

CONCLUSION

Heather Hart

Beauty. It isn't what's on the outside – it isn't just one thing at all. A girl that's truly beautiful will be a reflection of Christ. Knowing that she is cherished and accepted by God, she will remain pure as the bride of Christ. She will work diligently for His glory. Her true beauty will be displayed not by clothes, but by the words that come out of her mouth. It will shine through the way she treats others.

Being beautiful in Christ isn't as easy as slapping on a layer of makeup in the morning or making sure to pick up the right clothes when you're at the mall – it takes a commitment and the help of Christ living within you. It isn't something that you can achieve on your own, but it's a beauty that surpasses any physical primping you could ever do.

We hope the prayers you've read in this book have helped you draw closer to God and to deepen your true beauty in Christ.

"Praise be to God, who has not rejected my prayer or withheld His love from me!"

~Psalm 66:20 (NIV)

SCRIPTURES ON PRAYER

"The sacrifice of the wicked is an abomination to the Lord,
But the prayer of the upright is His delight."
~ Proverbs 15:8 (NASB)

"And all things you ask in prayer, believing, you will receive."
~ Matthew 21:22 (NASB)

"Be joyful in hope, patient in affliction, faithful in prayer."
~ Romans 12:12 (NIV)

"And pray in the Spirit on all occasions with all kinds of prayers
and requests. With this in mind, be alert and always keep on
praying for all the saints."
~ Ephesians 6:18 (NIV)

"Devote yourselves to prayer with an alert mind and a thankful
heart."
~ Colossians 4:2 (NLT)

"I urge, then, first of all, that requests, prayers, intercession and
thanksgiving be made for everyone."
~1 Timothy 2:1 (NIV)

"During the days of Jesus' life on earth, e offered up prayers and
petitions with loud cries and tears to the One who could save Him
from death, and He was heard because of His reverent
submission."
~ Hebrews 5:7 (NIV)

"Is anyone among you suffering? Then he must pray. Is anyone cheerful? He is to sing praises."

~ James 5:13 (NASB)

"and the prayer offered in faith will restore the one who is sick, and the Lord will raise him up, and if he has committed sins, they will be forgiven him."

~ James 5:15 (NASB)

"do not be anxious about anything, but in everything by prayer and supplication with thanksgiving let your requests be made known to God."

~ Philippians 4:6 (ESV)

Suggested Resources

More Books From FindYourTrueBeauty.com:

"Mirror Mirror... Am I Beautiful?" -
http://www.amazon.com/dp/B0046A9LVE/

21 Teen Devotionals... For Girls! –
http://www.amazon.com/dp/B009JU23IE/

Teen Devotionals... For Girls! Vol. 1-
http://www.findyourtruebeauty.com/devo-kindle

Teen Devotionals... For Girls! Vol. 2 -
http://amzn.to/teendevoskindle2

Live Without Stress: 30 days to finding Christ's peace for your soul. - http://bit.ly/LiveWithoutStress

Body Image Lies Women Believe -
http://www.amazon.com/dp/B00B9MZIEG

Bible Reading Plans:

YouVersion - http://www.youversion.com/reading-plans/all
BibleGateway - http://www.biblegateway.com/reading-plans/

CONTACT INFORMATION

We would love to hear from you!
To share your thoughts or read what
others had to say, please visit:

www.FindYourTrueBeauty.com

You can also send us an e-mail or a letter to one of the following address:

heather@teen-beauty-tips.com

Body and Soul Publishing
P.O. Box 6542
Colorado Springs, Colorado 80934

WEBSITES:
www.findyourtruebeauty.com
www.bodyandsoulpublishing.com

CJ AND SHELLEY HITZ

CJ and Shelley Hitz enjoy sharing God's Truth through their speaking engagements and their writing. On downtime, they enjoy spending time outdoors running, hiking and exploring God's beautiful creation.

To find out more about their ministry or to invite them to your next event, check out their websites:

www.BodyandSoulPublishing.com
www.ChristianSpeakers.tv

Note from the Author: Reviews are gold to authors! If you have enjoyed this book, would you consider reviewing it on Amazon.com? Thank you!

GET OUR OTHER DEVOTIONAL BOOKS

90 Devotionals to Encourage and Inspire You!

Teen Devotionals...
for Girls!

Written by Shelley Hitz, Heather Hart
and Contributing Authors

Brought to You By:
Find your true *Beauty*.com

Get FREE Teen Devotionals for Girls Here:
www.findyourtruebeauty.com/devos

Made in the USA
San Bernardino, CA
23 November 2018